Season of Singleness:

*Reward of Overcoming the Struggle of an
Absentee Father to Accepting
The Genuine Father's Love*

Season of Singleness:

*Reward of Overcoming the Struggle of an
Absentee Father to Accepting
The Genuine Father's Love*

Ciarra Leathers

*Kingdom Impactors Publishing
Houston, Texas
2012*

Season of Singleness: Reward of Overcoming the Struggle of an Absentee Father to Accepting The Genuine Father's Love

Please note that it is the practice of Kingdom Impactors Publishing to capitalize certain pronouns in Scripture and the author's writing that refer to God, the Father, Son, and Holy Spirit and may differ from the styles of other publishers.

Some names and identifying details have been changed to protect the privacy of individuals.

Published by Kingdom Impactors Publishing
P. O. Box 35708
Houston, Texas 77235-5708
Printed in the United States of America

ISBN 978-0-9822334-0-5

To God

My Savior, My Redeemer, my Husband,

my Spiritual Lover and Leader ...

I love that I am no longer empty, but defined in You.

TABLE OF CONTENTS

Foreword   XI

Innocent   1

Can You See Abandonment?   3

Overview of the Book   5

Unknown   7

Chapter 1: Absent Father   9

Chapter 2: A Turn for the Worse   13

Chapter 3: Low Self-Esteem: A Dark Girl in a Light World   17

Chapter 4: Emptied All Out   19

Chapter 5: Transitioning Period–The Day I Met My Savior   27

Chapter 6: How Could You?   29

Chapter 7: An On-Going Period of Restoration   37

Chapter 8: Obedience Through God's Love   41

Chapter 9: Dying to be Free   43

Chapter 10: My Moment of Silence   45

Chapter 11: My Season of Singleness   49

Chapter 12: A Period of Forgiveness   51

Chapter 13: As You Wait On Your Boaz   57

Chapter 14: Things to Consider Rather Than – Why Me?   61

Chapter 15: Support & Accountability From Friends & Family   63

Chapter 16: My Letter to God   71

Afterword   73

About The Author   75

Acknowledgements   77

Appendix 1   81

Appendix 2   85

Suggested Reading   93

Hotlines   95

x

FOREWORD

*S*eason of Singleness is a powerful story about a promising young woman that will resonate with many - an absent father, a broken home, a misguided life… Singleness is a gift that too few understand. And because it is not understood it is not valued. And because it is not valued it is not protected. As a matter of fact, our culture idolizes impurity and immorality. We are ambushed daily with images which reinforce the values of a hedonistic culture. But, you hold in your hand a book that challenges these cultural values.

Season of Singleness is a must read for all who find themselves at the crossroads of guilt and shame. The author speaks candidly of her own painful past. She is transparent about her own troubled life. But through it all she reminds us that true worth is not found in a man or mere human pursuits but in God.

Season of Singleness is a must read for every child who was raised without the active presence of a father in their life, every young person struggling with their sexuality and identity, and every person trying to navigate their way through despair, pain, and loneliness. The author points us to another road where we can find hope, help, and healing.

Several years ago Ciarra joined the church where I was pastoring. I had the joy of baptizing her into the Beacon Light Seventh-day Adventist Church and to watch her grow and blossom into the fine Christian woman that she is today. Had Ciarra not opened her heart towards a forgiving and loving God her story might be quite different. But glory to God, what began with an absent earthly father ended with an ever present heavenly Father.

Season of Singleness will make you want to cry, but it will make you hope again. Most of all, it will encourage you to put your trust in the only one who can truly satisfy and fulfill your deepest needs.

Dr. Compton Ross, Jr.

Departmental Director Central States Conference of Seventh-day Adventists

Kansas City, KS

INNOCENT

An Innocent child, with an innocent sense,
All the child ever wanted was to love two parents
That loved her back.

But even before she had a chance to live life
Her dad took it from her and denied her,
Denied her, her right to have a father.

But still the child is just as innocent
Still so young and unaware,
Unaware that her dad puts her on hold.
Rather party than spend time with her.

An innocent child that only wanted a chance,
A chance to experience love like no other love.

But again a boy, I say a boy because if he was any kind of
man
He wouldn't run and hide,
From a responsibility he had part of.

Now an innocent soul,
Must face the fact of a dad who does not love her.
How would she understand?
How would a child take this news?

He should have been there,
If he was any kind of father
He wouldn't have to choose.

W hen a baby is born, it cries out for attention, attention of some human form it can attach to and feel loved. If a baby has no form of attachment at birth, the little child cannot survive. A baby's human existence is based on affection and the touch of another human life. Without the bond of a human figure the baby cannot exist and without the bond of a father the child may never know his or her value.

My journey began with an absent father which left me feeling abandoned. I realized I needed help but I denied the way I felt because I allowed my pain to guide me instead of allowing God to direct my path. I longed to feel loved and appreciated. In this longing I allowed men to use me in a way that demeaned me as a woman. It left me broken, uncertain and in a whole lot of pain. A friend once said to me, "How can you not see your worth and allow such foolishness to overtake you," but like that newborn baby who could not exist without human touch I thought I could not exist without a man.

Can You See Abandonment?

What Does God See?

OVERVIEW OF THE BOOK

This book will uncover some of my darkest secrets and some of my lowest points, but it also offers hope. The importance of this book is for everyone to know that their true worth is not found in man but God, Who guides our steps and directs our path. Some of the things I will share will be deeply personal. Some of it may be difficult for you to read. This book depicts a journey through my life of loneliness and despair.

For years, I filled myself with "men" who left me drained and spiritually sick. I did not know how to love myself, or allow another human being to love me. I filled myself with lies from the enemy, and allowed him to prey on my weaknesses. The overwhelming desire to feel wanted and love led me to look for attention in all the wrong places and from the wrong men. When I lost the strength to fight, God reminded me that the battle I faced was not mine but His. He led me to a scripture –

Stand still and know that I am God.

Psalm 46:10

Each lesson was painful. Every subsequent abandonment left me hurt and alone. Finally, I learned:

When God removes people of significance from your life, the detachment is so powerful it feels as if you are being betrayed; but, you are not. You are being strengthened.

It is not God's will for me to be paralyzed by the pain of my past. He has plans for good and not for disaster, to give me a future and a hope (Jeremiah 29:11 NLT). I believe they will one day include a husband. I do desire to get married; but before I can be completely submissive to my husband, I have to be completely submissive to Jesus Christ. I am still learning this. I still struggle with internal issues that only God can help me through. Since I was never taught the proper way to love, God is teaching me how to love Him. In the midst of me loving Him, I am growing to love and value myself. God is molding and shaping me into the woman that He loves - me.

The *Season of Singleness* is not meant for one to be alone, but to be content with your alone time in Christ before you can give yourself completely to another person. Paul said it best in Philippians 4:12 NIV, "I know what it is to be in need, and I know what it is to have plenty. I have learned the secret of being content in any and every situation, whether well fed or hungry, whether living in plenty or in want." I had to learn like Paul to be content with Christ before I can learn how to love someone else. Through the struggles I faced I was able to fall to my knees and become vulnerable to the one man that always mattered – Jesus Christ.

> *Even though I walk through the valley of the shadow of death, I will fear no evil, for you are with me; your rod and your staff, they comfort me.*

> ***Psalm 23:4***

UNKNOWN

I was born into this world on April 26, not knowing what the future held. The delivery room was filled with the joy of a mother but the father was absent. The bond of a male figure never existed. As a little girl, at age 5, I thought that this world only existed to girls, and I did not realize my worth. I ended up allowing people to sexually exploit me, and for the longest I thought this was normal. My innocence was lost long before I reached puberty. When I became of age I was disgusted with myself and my father for not setting an example of how little girls are supposed to act. My mother did all she could, but with other children in the home, she could not focus on the one that was already so far gone. I lost myself long before I was able to understand what being a human was. I was robbed of my childhood, as if it were taken from me at birth.

My behavior in public places and school reflected the sexual abuse, but I was ashamed at the thought of telling anyone. I would cover up my dark secret for years and bury it in a place where only darkness lies.

It was only as I grew older that it became clear to me that God wanted me to share my story, the agony, along with the pain. Many people could not understand how I could survive such devastating events. My life has become a mere miracle of how God can use someone whose life was upside down and turn it right side up.

Now I can understand how I survived through these dark stages of my life. It is because my Heavenly Father through His mercy and grace thought more of me than I ever had thought of myself. He was protecting me long before I ever knew Him.

As you read this book ask yourself have you ever allowed your past to dictate your future? Have you ever been lost in a dark place and the only way out is through suicide, alcohol, drugs and sex at whatever cost?

God wants you to know that you are better than what the enemy is trying to place on you. Through my life experiences both good and horrible, I have learned that this was the life I was dealt. I had a choice to either throw in the towel, or grow where I was planted. By the grace of God I decided to begin where I was. I knew it would not be easy, and that I would face many challenges. I am finally beginning to see that I have made the right choice to not live my life on failed expectations.

My prayer is that everyone who reads this book will receive a renewed heart and a better understanding of their value and worth.

CHAPTER 1

ABSENT FATHER

Be strong and courageous. Do not be afraid or terrified because of them, for the LORD your God goes with you; he will never leave you nor forsake you.

Deuteronomy 31:6

I grew up in a troubled home. My mother loved me dearly but I did not have a father. My biological father was in and out my life. His mother, my paternal grandmother, took the bulk load of his responsibility toward me. She would buy gifts and say they were from him. Imagine the anger and disappointment I must have felt.

My mother had already dealt with so much in her own life. Before I was born she had to deal with my biological father's lies, after-hours spent with different women and neglect toward her. His lies even led to my mother having altercations with his other women. Although they were not married and I was a born out of wedlock, my mother had no right to be disrespected. Selfish and inconsiderate, he was in my opinion a womanizer, philanderer of the worst kind.

When I was one year old, my father was shot at close range in the neck when caught with another woman. Luckily my father survived, but he was paralyzed from the neck down. I have chosen to believe that God gave him a second chance. The bullet caused the loss the mobility of his lower body. In my mind it seemed as if God was trying to tell him, "I am in control; you manipulated women for too long. It is time you feel how degraded those women must have felt, and to see your fault and see what it is like not having the use of what has destroyed many countless women." Break dancing was his thing. This is how he would lure women and rob them of the small amount of dignity they had. One might think that not being able to move would have given him time to reflect on his actions. It did not; he was worse off than before.

At some point, his mother thought that the turn of events due to his injury would be a good bonding time for us because his circumstance offered no other choice but to be in my life now. However, I was faced with a dilemma. How can a man that has never been in my life expect me to call him "daddy?" When I did not oblige to addressing him as "daddy," he would get angry. I believed I was being forced to use a term of endearment he did not deserve.

So my mother finally sent me to live with my father and his mother. I felt imprisoned. I could not talk to my friends on the phone, and I was allowed to talk to my mother only once a day. Outdoors was off limits unless I was accompanied by an adult. At the age of 13, my father told me that I was a mistake at birth and would never amount to anything because I was too fast. He stated that I did not deserve to be loved and he could not see how he could make such a child. He never cared for children, not even his own. I felt the neglect that was put upon me by my biological father because I never experienced love from him.

CHAPTER 2

A TURN FOR THE WORSE

In my neglect, in an unfamiliar household, I started to doubt myself, I had low self-esteem and insecurities, I even thought about suicide. I started to act out to receive the attention I was not receiving from him. Knowing the rules of the home, one night I decided to sneak on the phone to call my mother although I had already talked with her earlier, I was caught and my punishment was to sit in the room with him for hours not saying a word, I could not even use the bathroom. I spent many nights like this and I was tired, so I ran away one night barefooted in the rain. I had to get away from the imprisonment I felt.

The one place I went for help killed what was left in me. I was sexually assaulted by my cousin, a man I trusted who was much older than I was. He touched me in places that brought back memories to my early childhood. He made me touch him in places that scarred me for life, and forced me to do unspeakable things. When I sought help from my paternal grandmother, she shunned me, and I lost hope. I never had someone I could spill out this pain to, who could see through the pain I felt growing up. This turn sent my whole world crashing down and this was the beginning to an even deeper darkness.

Left Abandoned

I no longer trusted anyone in my life. Although I was no longer staying with my biological father, I had become an out of control teen. I got arrested for assault and was sent to juvenile for a week. My body became art work, every chance I got I tattooed and pierced wherever I could. I started dating a guy who was a known drug dealer. He would take me on "serves" with him. In the hood, they called it "busting serves." I was the look out; they never would expect a female so young. I was turned out at an early age.

Soon I started hanging around the wrong crowd of "friends," wearing provocative clothes, drinking, and partying. My first club experience was at age 14 with my cousin, I dressed provocatively in order to gain attention from the men around me. My body was no longer mine; I did not care what happened to it because it was taken from me long before I had a choice. I would let men degrade me on the dance floor because I had given up on myself. Of course I had to be drunk, so I would consume three beers or something that was 151 proof so I could not have any recollection of my actions. The drinking took away the pain and recognition of who I was. I was a lost teenage girl with no hope, my innocence taken from me and my name smeared. I remembered thinking I was born to be a disappointment. Not only was my biological father out of my life, but I was left abandoned at the time I needed him the most.

Eventually, I realized that I had a serious problem with drinking when I consumed three beers within one hour. Camos was my beer of choice because they were cheap and hardcore. This was the next best thing to malt liquor. I would drink alcohol to the point where I was numb and unresponsive.

One New Year's Eve, I got wasted with some friends. Because we were not of legal drinking age, my friend's brother had to purchase the alcohol for us. We had no particular preference, just be any dark liquor. Rum was one of my favorites. We started drinking about 7:00 PM. We were never the type to mix liquor with juice. We were hardcore drinkers, and would mix liquor with other liquors. The whole point of this was to be so far gone that we were beyond drunk. We ended at about 2:30am. By that time I had passed out and woke up with a hangover.

This behavior went on for months. It became a part of our weekends. We would drink. Others would smoke and we all would hit the clubs. The club scene was our spot; it was our way of meeting men in order to get them to buy us more liquor. We were a pretty wild bunch. This type of rebellion went on for a couple of years.

Then I received a phone call on March 26, 2000, my uncle called and the first words he said to me were "sorry to hear about your dad." WHAT! All of my rebellion was an act to get my father's attention, but now he was gone. I went to the funeral but did not mourn. It was then that I realized that I never needed his approval.

My identity was not in him. Whether he lived or died it was not going to fix anything. I wish I could tell you after that realization that I stopped searching for my father's love. But, I didn't. I wish I could tell you that I learned how to love myself. But, I couldn't.

CHAPTER 3
LOW SELF-ESTEEM: A DARK GIRL IN A LIGHT WORLD

I can remember the day I first noticed I was dark. I was in middle school and a kid referred to me as "darky." I went home the next day and tried scrubbing my face until I realized my skin color was permanent. I was so hurt. Any small amount of confidence that I had was gone. I felt unaccepted and unloved. I cried for hours. I was dealing with this type of judgment my school and my own family.

My complexion was always a problem to me; I felt I had to work twice as hard to get attention. I remember going on a blind-date with a friend and my blind-date was light skinned. He took one look at me and said, "Usually I don't do dark girls, but you are cute to be dark, I will make an exception for you." When he said that it pierced my heart and it brought me right back to that painful day in middle school. I'm embarrassed to admit that I continued to date the guy, and every time I was with him he made me feel worse off than the last time. It was cold outside and I was freezing, and he said, "that's because you're dark." Trying to recover the pieces of my childhood with an absent father was difficult now that I was dealing with insecurity issues due to my skin tone. Another nightmare of being dark was the memory of buying fade cream, fade soap and whatever else I could think of that would lighten my skin. I would not go swimming, and I only went outside when the sun went down. I would not date dark skin men because I was afraid of having dark children. I was brained washed by society to think my own appearance was "ugly."

I felt empty inside, and everything in my life was cursed at this point. I felt worse than Job.

CHAPTER 4

EMPTIED ALL OUT

For a long time I felt unworthy of God's blessings. I was this empty child with no hope or direction. I thought I could fill the emptiness with a man. Since my father was deceased there was emptiness in my heart from wanting to experience a father's love. I could not have him so I put men in his place.

Next are accounts of some of those "fillers" that entered and exited my life. **Please, note:** The names have been changed to conceal their true identities. At this printing, each are aware of this book being written to assist in the healing and deliverance of its readers. If there are any similarities in any of your relationships, please heed the signs and run. If you are like the men, stop and seek counsel for change.

Allan, the Charmer

I met Allan while I was on spring break from school. I was with my cousin at the gas station and He approached me, I remember thinking, "he is too little" but he was so cute; a pretty boy might I add. He approached me in such a respectful and polite manner. I had to give him my phone number. He called me the same night. We talked on the phone for hours getting to know one another. We had a few things in common, and it felt good to focus my attention on one person. I felt like he was genuine. Although, I had this rule that any guy I talk to had to go through my friends, especially Andrea. She was a tough cookie. If he passed her grilling, he was a keeper. He passed, and by this time we had gotten serious. He introduced me to his mother and we were together all the time, if not, most of his days were spent with me. Things were finally looking up. I was finally happy. Nothing could knock me off the high horse I was on.

Conformity

I was finally with a guy that didn't pressure me for sex, didn't ask me for anything, and just loved being in my presence or so I thought. Then the day came when he stopped returning phone calls, and he was never at home. I remember thinking how could something that started off so perfect end so hurtful.

A few months passed then I got a call, "I'm sorry, I tried working it out with my baby momma for the sake of our daughter, but it didn't work out, can you forgive me?" Like a fool, I forgave him because emotionally I was still tied to the false hope this man was giving me.

For a while it was different, for a while it was better, he seemed to be a great guy. He would call me just to check in, before and after work. He would only allow his daughter to come visit him, instead of him visiting her; simply because he knew I was uncomfortable with the former. I thought he was doing all of this out of an act of love, so everything he wanted me to change I did. I would not wear weave because he hated "fake" hair. I would not wear nails because he preferred my natural nails. I was falling for this guy, this time even harder than before.

When I decided to tell him how I felt, he had nothing to say. I was shocked and surprised because his actions told me something totally different. After a long period of silence, "Thank you," that is what he said to me. I had just opened up my heart and the only words he could say were thank you? I did not know how to react so I just changed the subject and pretended it never happened. That day was the last time I heard from him.

After months of pain and crying I realized he never cared. I had never met his daughter, and the only reason I ever met his mother is because he was living with her. The most important person in his life, his daughter, I was not ever introduced to her. I discovered that the reason I never met his daughter is because he did not completely leave his "baby momma" alone. They were still pretty much an item. I never put it together at the time. Few years later, he contacted me to apologize, by this time I had moved on but so had he.

After Allan I was still empty. One may think that I would have learned from Allan, but I would continue to search for love in all the wrong places.

Chad, The Slick-Talker

Chad had a certain swagger that was attractive to me. This is a demeanor that I did not see in Allan. Chad also loved sports. I seemed to be attracted to ruthless dudes. Maybe because my father depicted all of that kind of "thug life" that seems appealing. I just could not see past this into reality.

Chad and I met at school where we would chat about sports highlights. One day we decided to catch a game together. I knew he was not the relationship type, but I was cool with that, I just wanted a friend. We started hanging out and hanging out turned into something more. We got physical not to the point of sex but close. He respected the fact that I would not have sex although he wanted to. We had a dysfunctional relationship. Although I was not "his girl," I still didn't want him talking to any other girl. He thought I was delusional and said, "You're not putting out so what you tripping on?" I couldn't believe he said that to me but I respected his honesty. Although I knew he was sleeping with other girls and coming to lay with me in the bed, I was cool with that. He was the rudest, disrespectful guy I had ever met outside of my father, and I still wanted him around.

Rock Bottom

Chad was not the type that showed affection, and he did not like spending money on females, but he did not mind them spending money on him. I can recall an incident when we were intoxicated; I think I may have wanted to drink more than him because I knew that was his thing. I was in his room knocking down cups and cups of Remy. I just remember being dizzy and throwing up, and everything from there went blank. I do remember waking up in my own room, and hurting vaginally. He called the next morning, and said he had to put me out because I was tripping and could not handle my liquor. I asked him if anything sexual had happened between us and he denied it. I did not see him as the rapist type; although I did not put anything pass him. In retrospect I probably should have gone to the hospital for an exam, but I did not. I could not recall anything. I just wasn't sure. He had no right to take advantage of me, but at the time I was not thinking about this, all I wanted was the attention. While this was the wrong kind of attention it was still attention. I continued talking to him. The more time I spent with him the worse I would feel. Looking back I can see he was using me, I did not see this until the day came that I needed him and he did not come through for me.

Lonnie, The Con-Artist

After graduating I tried to convince myself that I was through talking to "no good" guys. I was tired of being strung along and used. Then I met Lonnie, it was out of the blue, he was a friend of my cousin. I would visit my cousin often and Lonnie was always around. My cousin introduced us. Lonnie was a deacon, a man of God. I never had one of those before. He seemed like a pretty cool guy. I never knew he had an underlying motive. Every time I would visit my cousin he would show up randomly. I never thought anything of it until it all blew up in my face.

There were days I would come over and he would make it his business to come outside whenever I would drive up. He would come to my car and talk to me for hours. He even told me about his prior incidents with females and how they got too deep into their feelings for him. One female he was messing with keyed his car because after leading her on, he moved on. I did not take the keyed car as a sign. Nor did I run. Because I did not know any better at the time, due to never being taught and was still looking for love.

> *When God gives you signs, please take heed and RUN.*

Lonnie and I started talking on the phone, nothing serious just friendly conversations- getting to know one another, small talk things. I thought, "This guy is a man of God and could finally be what I've been looking for!" One day he accompanied me to one of my best friend's album release party. We would hang out with friends, things were looking up for me but I was blind to the signs. Everywhere we went I asked him to accompany me, but he never invited me anywhere. All I saw was what I wanted to see: us praying on the phone together after conversations, our talks about relationships, and him casually checking up on me throughout the day. I thought this man was too good to be true.

One night I wanted company and asked him if I could come over to his house. He said, "Yeah, sure." It was late at night when I arrived at his house, and that night ended sexually charged. We did not have sexual intercourse, but we engaged in highly sexual activity. Sadly, I thought this was love. After that night I was hooked and so was he - so I thought. He was going out of town that following week so he said we were going to hook up when he got back. Everything seemed normal up until he got back. He did not call when he returned. It was then that I discovered that he was in another relationship.

I was beyond hurt. I felt he led me on. How could he lie to me? I thought, "What If he would have been honest?" Looking back, I can see now that there were plenty of signs, but I just chose to ignore them. I called him because I was upset, and he said to me, "I'm sorry, this relationship I'm in - kind of just happened. I still would like us to be friends though." I cried and cried. Sadly, not only did I open myself up to get hurt, but I was blinded to the truth.

Defining Moment

Many other incidents with males took place. I was still looking for a superman to fill all the hurt I was feeling toward my father. Unhealthy emotions festered which allowed more unhealthy relationships. Many boundaries were crossed. I admit that I was needy. I was ready to pick up the pieces of my life. I knew that nothing would be the same, but I never lost hope because I believed in new beginnings.

Eye Opening

I never learned how to love myself. All I really needed to *know* was the man – JESUS- who was ready to fulfill all of my deepest hurts and desires, but until I met Him I was always going to be **empty**.

CHAPTER 5
TRANSITIONING PERIOD – THE DAY I MET MY SAVIOR

For in this hope we were saved. But hope that is seen is no hope at all. Who hopes for what they already have? But if we hope for what we do not yet have, we wait for it patiently.

Romans 8:24-25

My transition from my troubled youth officially started when I was introduced to the Seventh Day Adventist (SDA) church in Kansas City, Missouri, by my best friend Victoria. I walked in the church a filthy rag, filled with lies and deception and came out cleansed with the truth. I finally felt like I had a purpose on this earth. I was baptized on August 14, 2004; I realized that God had chosen me like He chose Noah, Abraham, Isaac, Jacob, Peter, and Paul. I felt at home, the SDA church became my home and family.

My mother and Aunt Carolyn supported me as I took the huge step to attend college, going beyond what others in my family thought possible. I am the first person in my immediate family to attend college and graduate. I knew my past was the least of my worries and my future held my story. There are people out in this world who share the same story as me. I did not attempt to fill the shoes left behind by others in my family. I have made my own shoes and blazed my own trail. This is important because I needed to understand that just because I came from a troubled childhood, I didn't have to let that define who I am today. I needed to go beyond what people thought of me.

Pursuing a BA in English with an emphasis on Journalism was brought about when I noticed my talent for writing. While I was growing up I had turned to writing as a coping skill to deal with my problems. My writing pad was my counselor. I became a true survivor and I faced my biggest fear-my past.

> *I don't mean to say that I have already achieved these things or that I have already reached perfection! But I keep working toward that day when I will finally be all that Christ Jesus saved me for and wants me to be. No, dear brothers and sisters, I am not all I should be, but I am focusing all my energies on this one thing: Forgetting the past and looking forward to what lies ahead, I strain to reach the end of the race and receive the prize for which GOD, through CHRIST JESUS, is calling us up to HEAVEN (emphasis added)."*

> *Philippians 3:12-14 NLT*

CHAPTER 6

HOW COULD YOU?

I had written men off. I had found an even greater love, Jesus. I was no longer looking but I still felt empty. I had moved to Houston, Texas, and had a new focus of growing in Christ. I was introduced to the music ministry in Houston, although I was familiar with it back at home in Kansas City. This was something I loved doing - spreading the Gospel of Christ. I was a manager so my role was to branch out and help other artists. I loved it. I love supporting people who are on fire for Christ.

Downfall

It was not long until another obstacle approached. I did not know it was going to be this steep, but God had to show me. I met Gabe, a gospel artist who ministered through Christian rap. We were nothing but friends; I never looked at him more than just a brother in Christ. We started going on road trips together for the ministry and that is when our relationship turned into something more.

During a trip back home, a playful act turned into something that would later put our souls in jeopardy. We started touching each other's hands, and that led to something we both were not prepared for. I thought that the incident was over, but then he called me a few days later and brought it up. I knew my past, my struggles, and all of the emptiness and I did not want to play with fire again. How could I? I was saved now. We both decided to put the incident behind us.

We became real close friends, he would confide in me about his relationship that was not going well, I would try to give him the best advice a friend could give. We were something like "best friends." Those were his words, not mine. We would talk on the phone often. Shorter conversations turned into longer conversations that turned into all night conversations. Everything we discussed on the phone was biblical - nothing inappropriate. We were just really good friends that enjoyed one another's conversation.

One night we were talking, I had just left school around 10:30 PM and he suggested that I come visit him. There were so many signs from God that told me to say NO. God was telling me that you know what you have been delivered from, why go back down that same road? I tuned Him out and I thought, we are just friends and he is already in a relationship with someone else. What could possibly happen? I told him that I would be there but I had to make a stop first, that stop lasted longer than I expected. During my stop Gabe would text me and ask was I still coming. By this time it was approaching 12:00 AM, I answered him back telling him I would be there. I knew I was making the wrong decision, but I went anyway.

> **The timing (late night) should have been a wakeup call.**

The mind frame at that hour of the night could only be a lustful state. I knew I wasn't strong enough to face the temptations my flesh, but I acted upon my flesh anyway. I had ignored the Spirit of God.

My mind and spirit was not right when I arrived; I was already feeling lustful.

He invited me into his home and we sat on the coach watching television. The show we were watching was pretty funny. I remember soft laughter. I could feel the closeness. My body went with the only closeness I knew- *intimacy*. Then I kissed him. I know.

What I was thinking? When he did not kiss me back, I felt humiliated and ashamed. What did I just do? Everything going through my head was a replay, from the rejection I had received from my father and other men in my life. I kissed him again.

The one thing we both struggled with, the enemy used against us. My struggle was with men and his with women. After he had kissed me back, he said to me, "Are you sure you want to do this?" I was thinking NO, but my body said, "Yes, I am sure." We ended up at a hotel and I was willing to give myself to a man I barely knew. That night I lost myself. My dignity was gone. I cried out in his presence, we both did. Lord, forgive us. Although we had died that night to our flesh, we still had hope. After this event I could not bear to talk to him, I was mad at myself and ashamed of my lack of self-discipline. I wish I could tell you that it stopped here but it did not. I really tried to cut him loose but by then my emotions got involved.

> **God intended for sexual relations to be inside a marital covenant, not to limit us, but to protect us from emotional attachments, or soul-ties.**

Having any form of sexual relations, even acts other than intercourse, outside of marriage can cloud your judgment and make it even harder to resist temptation. A sexual demon is like a dark cloud that will never leave unless you are completely covered by the Word of God.

Gabe would not stop talking to me; he felt like he started something that was never finished. I was technically still a virgin, because he was unable to break my hymen.

Our conversations on the phone became the norm. We would argue as if we were in a meaningful relationship, but we were not. We would stay on the phone throughout the night until 6:00 the next morning. He would call me just to talk no matter what time it was.

He was talking to me more than he was talking to his girlfriend. By this time I started letting him in. He did the same. I knew this was not good.

He would get frustrated when I would not answer his calls. He would get mad when I tried to cut him off by not answering my phone. I know that probably was not the best way to go about not talking to him but that was the only way. He would text, leave messages, and for some reason I felt bad so many people had walked out on him and I did not want to be that person. This hotel thing became our normal routine, we both wanted sex. We never actually had sex during the first encounter. In retrospect, an important factor was that I had been sexually assaulted when I was younger. I was touched, fondled, but I had never been penetrated. So I was willing to share that with him. I grew an attachment to him, an emotional bond. He also opened himself up to me emotionally. He told me that he missed me and had grown to have feelings for me. I was so confused, all I could think of is he is in another relationship. How could we both feel this way? Somehow and some way I knew I had to stop talking to him.

The emotional attachment I had with Gabe had grown too strong. I had no choice but to cut off contact with him. Either I stay and drain myself physically or move along and gain myself spiritually. The right choice was to move forward. The realization had finally set in and the recovery process had begun. My thoughts were, "When God brings you out of something trust God to keep you out; because there is no way that God will send you someone with someone else in the way."

Finally, I had enough strength to text him my out, so I did: "During my fast, I had some time to think things over... for years I always took the easy way out just to finish quick but not this time I want to finish well. So with that being said, this chapter in my life is over. I'm not saying we can't be friends but at this point in my life I need my space. With our desire for attention the devil will use that desire to tempt us in areas we are most weak. I'm on a path to set healthy boundaries and grow in the areas where we both struggle-self-discipline. I made a bad decision and went about it the wrong way, but a part of growing is learning."

I felt relieved. He sent me a text back, "Amen, I pray your strength in the Lord."
WHAT? I expected a phone call or numerous text messages. I expected more than what he gave me because that was what I was accustomed to. I told myself things must have gotten better between him and his girlfriend. I allowed myself to heal, but deep down I was missing him like crazy.

One day, I decided to attend an event where he was scheduled to minister. This is when everything hit the fan. Then I knew he never cared for me. He walked in with another woman who lived overseas. This girl was not his girlfriend, but a girl he had met from a social networking site. I felt stupid and humiliated. It all made sense now, no wonder he did not care that I was leaving him alone, he had already moved on. All the time I spent pouring into him he was pouring into someone else. I was furious, I walked up to him and said, "so, you have been manipulating and lying this whole time." I turned and walked away. He came running after me but by this time I knew where God was leading me. Gabe gave me this sob story about them being just friends and that he never lied to me. Then he told me that I was blowing this out of proportion – even offering to bring the woman over so that I could ask her myself. At this point it did not matter.

He kept calling and texting me for some time, but at this point I was **finally finished**.

Eyes Opened

I almost lost myself hanging on to something I could not have. I could not blame Gabe; this whole time I felt God was saying to me, "You finally found me but you do not value me." I had the discernment but I chose not to act on it. The Lord had to show me where it painfully hurt. Believe me when I tell you God came through that night, He not only showed me that I did not value Him but that I am never going to move past this emptiness until I forgive the one person who I let cause my emptiness- my father.

Sadly, I realized that I never had an emotional bond or attachment toward my father. Maybe this is why I was becoming emotionally attached to these men. I wasted life being attached to these men when God was screaming, "I want to be your attachment, not a man, or your biological father. ME."

But God demonstrates his own love for us in this: While we were still sinners, Christ died for us.

Romans 5:8

The relationships with these men became a lustful desire - nothing more. I thought this was love because no one told me anything different. I remained in these relationships with unlovable types because I already knew what to expect. I had no sense of direction until I humbly chastised myself. I had no choice but to come to the Cross. I saw my sins placed upon Christ and knew that was "love." Love had no longer come in the form of "**lust**" but **chastity**. Through God sending His Son and by His stripes I was delivered.

But he was pierced for our transgressions,
he was crushed for our iniquities;
the punishment that brought us peace was on him,
and by his wounds we are healed.

Isaiah 53:5

CHAPTER 7

AN ON-GOING PERIOD OF RESTORATION

Neither height nor depth, nor anything else in all creation, will be able to separate us from the love of God that is in Christ Jesus our Lord.

Romans 8:39

The emptiness I felt having no father around growing up, and the type of attention I was receiving from men gave me no hope for tomorrow. However, there is no depth to which I could descend that God was not present. Even in my darkness God could not hide. Although I could not see or feel His presence, He did not abandon me. I would cry out to God in prayer, and He would hear me. Not even life's worst depression could separate me from the love of Christ. I am humble enough to admit that I allowed the wrong type of men in my life. Now I allow the Word to grow in me and never allow those types of men to pursue me because I have allowed God to pursue me instead.

Before, I saw my life as a means to an end. I had lost hope in everything so I gave my body away to men. I was angry that my biological father failed as a father and did not love me. I did not know how to express love to others. I thought I was unworthy of respect. How can any man love me if my father could not? Although my path seemed dim, I relied on the Word of God to see me through. Everything that was indifferent was reframed.

> *Come to me, all you who are weary and burdened, and I will give you rest. Take my yoke upon you and learn from me, for I am gentle and humble in heart, and you will find rest for your souls. For my yoke is easy and my burden is light.*
>
> *Matthew 11:28-30*

Then, I started looking at the tough times I faced with men differently. My biological father did not love me but my Heavenly Father loves me indeed. My biological father was not in my life but my Heavenly Father took His rightful place. My biological father failed as a father ,but where he failed God succeeded. My biological father caused me to search for love in men, but my only fulfillment can now come through Christ. I hated that I entertained the wrong type of men but God said, "Be patient and stop looking for your father in these men. I have already filled that void. I am your Father."

Believing that the ultimate purpose in life rests in God, I persevered.

I spent most of my years not forgiving my negligent biological father which led me to selfishness.

No one could please me, until I found Christ. Through my relationship with Christ I lost my selfishness and gained restoration which led to self respect and self-love.

> *Not only is this so, but we also boast in God through our Lord Jesus Christ, through whom we have now received reconciliation.*

Romans 5:11

CHAPTER 8

OBEDIENCE THROUGH GOD'S LOVE

For God so loved the world that he gave his one and only Son, that whoever believes in him shall not perish but have eternal life.

John 3:16

It should never take worldly pursuits to enhance a spiritual relationship with God. God alone should be the reason. I had to learn this the hard way, but I am glad that I did. Through everything that I learn about myself, the one thing that Christ desires me to abide by is something I fall short of daily, "love." Love is something I have struggled with because of my influences in this world. However, God repeatedly shows "love" throughout the Bible. Christ was the perfect example. God sacrificed his Son so that everyone who believes in Him will inherit eternal life. God saw my needs and knew that I could not make it on my own. I needed Christ for growth. The love Christ shows is unconditional.

In finding myself, I can begin to understand the depth of love. Through Christ, He made love possible. Seasons that come from love are possible for everyone

(Rom. 5:5). Here are a few: forgiveness, patience, kindness, love for truth, love for justice, loyalty at any cost, belief in a person no matter what (1 Cor. 13:4-7). Loves does not produce anger, greed, envy, pride, lust, indifference, selfishness, or unforgiveness. I can now acknowledge my need for salvation and forgiveness. As one seeks God, His love becomes more familiar.

> *And hope does not put us to shame, because God's love has been poured out into our hearts through the Holy Spirit, who has been given to us.*

> **Romans 5:5 ESV**

CHAPTER 9

DYING TO BE FREE

And we all, who with unveiled faces contemplate the Lord's glory,
are being transformed into his image with ever-increasing glory,
which comes from the Lord, who is the Spirit.

2 Corinthians 3:18

Sometimes people have to break free from themselves to fully be used by God. I had to break free from every negative thing that was holding me back from God. Paul had to be freed from himself for God to use him (Act 9:17-18). Now, I have come to realize that I have been promised ultimate intimacy with God. But in order to receive this I had to allow God to take precedence in my life. This transformation took place through the grace of God and a repentant heart.

I have come to a point in my life where I know that becoming Christ-like is a continual process. My grandmother was a great influence. Either my actions can lead to redemption or it can separate me from God. I know all have fallen short but grace and mercy overshadows sin. Grace begins with God and is given freely by God. Grace cannot be earned. Grace is freely given (Eph. 2:8-9). It is by God's grace that Season of salvation is offered. There is nothing one can do to earn it. It must simply be received in "**faith**."

> *For it is by grace you have been saved, through faith—and this is not from yourselves, it is Season of God—not by works, so that no one can boast.*

> *Ephesians 2:8-9*

CHAPTER 10

MY MOMENT OF SILENCE

Never will I leave you; never will I forsake you.

Hebrews 13:5

It is easy for us to get so overwhelmed with the things that provide temporary pleasure in our lives that we forget about God. I have experienced this. It took me to merely lose myself again before I came to God in complete silence. I got tired of my same mess and the distraction I allowed to keep me from God. This moment of silence was refreshing. I knew I had so much to say to my Heavenly Father. I had been distant from Him for a while. My needs had become more important to me than being in His presence. I knew that my Father longed for the intimacy of hearing my conversation again.

As I took this long deep breath, and closed my eyes, I took a walk through a path that looked like it would never end, I was reminded of His Grace and Mercy (Heb. 4:16). As I continued walking along the path, I instantly felt the walk that Christ had to walk over 2,000 years ago (Matt. 27). I felt forgiveness and I cried out, "Dear Father thanks! Thanks for everything. Sorry! Sorry for everything. Forgiveness, please, please Father forgive."

At that moment I felt warmth, I knew than that Christ has never left me. I was crucified along that path (Gal. 2:20). I could not help but to smile and praise God for the fulfillment that He always has been able to give me. The fear of rejection and ridicule was no longer present because I knew that no matter how hopeless things seem, in Christ I had ultimate eternal hope. This time, I had FINALLY had enough; I cried out to God, "Lord, help me!"

My silence allowed me to just listen. I finally understood my purpose in God, to praise and worship Him. Although my life seemed dim, God never left me. I needed this silence to repent and come back to Christ again; my unrepentant heart rejected God and I remained in sin's grasp. My repentance that night led me to forgiveness of sin. My broken and contrite heart was willing to confess and repent of sin and brought me back to Christ - salvation. I knew the value of my life. I realized that the cross was an expression of the grace and kindness of God, the very promise of eternal life which the Word of God promises.

So many times in my life I thought I could not come to God because I feared His disapproval. God's heart breaks when we continue to grope along in sin. Not realizing that God knows my heart, and in the midst of my disappointments, God forgives. Instead of condemnation and punishment of death, God sent Christ in our place. God promises never to leave us or forsake us. It took silence for me to realize that Christ never left.

Understanding My Emotions

I know that I may not be able to change the tragic events that happened to me in my childhood; but, if I change my outlook, I can change my emotional responses to life. I'm choosing to now. I can no longer live this anxious-ambivalent life that I've lived for years. For years I struggled with attachment, which injured my relationships with others. Everything about my life was unhealthy because I allowed it to be. Now that I'm aware, I'm changing for the better.

A friend once told me, "God will never deliver us from our struggles until we are disgusted by them, instead of just being convicted by them. Conviction comes only because the Father lives in us, but deliverance can only happen if we allow it."

So I knew that I was disgusted with my issues involving men. Instead of flirting and entertaining it, I chose not to go through those unresolved issues for the rest of my life. Right at that moment, I was willing to sacrifice my life of poor choices in fleeting relationships for death and resurrection with Christ. I was "dying to live the life He intended for me to live - victoriously."

CHAPTER 11

MY SEASON OF SINGLENESS

My constant battle with my single life had paralyzed my relationship with Christ. I have struggled with focusing on His Word. At times, I have lost my direction and purpose in life and to trust in God to fulfill all of His promises. I know now that God can restore all that seems to be destroyed, if you allow Him.

Everyone is not meant to have a mate. Paul progressed in life without one, and his drive and will to be an effective Christian resulted in joy.

We are all born with a purpose, and everything that we do not understand about ourselves, we can find in Scripture. Through Scripture I was reminded that God's power is magnified through our weaknesses and infirmities, if we allow Him to work within us.

My realization set in when I had moments to reflect on the goodness of God and how I had been robbed by letting myself think otherwise. I no longer think I need a man in my life to be sufficient in Christ. I am already sufficient in Christ. Since God is my ultimate comfort, His Word is my greatest resource for comfort.

Nonetheless, I know that singleness is a spiritual grace ordained by God – for a season.

God looked at me and saw my real worth, and now I know my true worth is **only** in Christ. I am content to live my life as a single woman – for now. That is until God, by His Spirit, and confirmation by wise counsel, directs me otherwise.

CHAPTER 12

A PERIOD OF FORGIVENESS

*And when you stand praying, if you hold anything against anyone,
forgive him, so that your Father in heaven may forgive you your sins.*

Mark 11:25

For the longest time, I did not know how to forgive my father. How could I forgive a man that had so much animosity in his heart toward me? Every part of me hated him for what he had done. I blamed him for every problem I faced with "no good" men. Then I realized that harboring unforgiveness only damages me. I thought about it and realized if I am trying to be like Jesus, then I will be treated like Him.

The Bible reminds us that our battle is not against flesh and blood, but it is a spiritual battle. The battle that has been raging is against people, but it is spiritual. This thought made it easier for me to overlook and forgive the fault.

Letter to My Dad

Every girl imagines her father teaching her about boys, teaching her manners and how to act appropriately as a growing woman. Every girl imagines her father running away guys she dates because they still cannot amount to Dad's expectations. Every girl imagines her father walking her down the aisle and giving her away at her wedding. Every girl imagines being daddy's little girl.

For years I wasted my life being mad at you. You had power over me even in the grave. I no longer want to harbor these feelings of hatred toward you. As a child I gave my heart to you and never got it back. I almost lost myself completely hanging on to all the "whys." Why couldn't you love me? Why did you hate me so much? Why was it so difficult to love me? I would cry every night wanting my father there. I spent half of my life searching for you in men, living in hurt and unbearable pain. They turned out to be just like you, they couldn't love either.

Wow, now as I look back I was trying to receive love from mean, demeaning, thoughtless, unlovable men. I was trying to receive love from you. For a long time I thought I was unworthy of real love, so I would do everything to sabotage it. I wasn't thankful, I would bore easily, I would constantly compete with other females and always praised attention from men. The one thing I absolutely hated about myself, was that I don't give myself easily, you taught me that. I have ruined some good relationships because of you. I can no longer live like this and continue to let you have this hold over me.

I forgive you and I don't blame you anymore. Everything negative you said to me was a lie. I am an amazing woman with a bright future. I no longer envy father and daughter relationships because I have a Father who has never left me. God is teaching me not only how to love, but how to be loved.

Letter To My Paternal Grandmother

I have always wondered what I might say to you given the chance to completely open up and be honest. Here it goes. You taught me to be a dominant and controlling woman. I still live by that to this day. It has not gotten me far –just, alone. I have accepted this. You were there when my father wasn't, and I am appreciative. However, I could never understand why you would make excuses for him. Now I get it, he was your only son. A part of me hated you because he was no longer here for me to hate. I didn't understand why you treated me like a prisoner instead of your granddaughter.

You thought you could buy my love, but my love was never for sale. I needed more than money; you missed the most important days of my life: my high school graduation, my awards ceremonies, my birthdays and my college graduation.

The day that really scarred me was when I told you I was sexually assaulted by my cousin and you said I was lying. How could you take away the ounce of hope that I had? How could you call me a liar? I had to live with the pain and agony that night brought. I still live with it. I want you to know what that night did to me. It took away my ability to trust, my self-worth— it took away me. You allowed a grown man to completely degrade and destroy a child. I wanted to die, but killing myself would have been useless because inside I was already dead. As a little girl I looked up to you only to be betrayed by you. I forgive you and I no longer blame you.

Letter To My Cousin

I thought I would never be able to forgive you. I thought when I had the chance to express myself I would curse you with hate. I hated the sight of you and the misery you put me through. I came to you for help and comfort at a time that I needed you most. You not only took away pieces of my childhood, you left me scarred and confused. I grew up with a lack of confidence. Alcohol became my closest friend. I went to bed with nightmares and alcohol was the only thing I knew at the time that would erase that awful night. I was ANGRY! I wanted every part of you to suffer because of what you did to me. After knowing Christ, I can forgive you. I forgive you for what you did to me that night. I just hope and pray you get right in your heart. I pray that you will repent and God will restore your heart.

The same salvation and restoration I pray for my cousin is available for everyone, no matter what. It is a gift. Just read what follows.

How to Come to Christ

- Repent of your sins. Change your mind set about how you do things. (Acts 3:19)
- Ask Jesus Christ, the Son of God to come into your life and believe in Him. (John 3:16)
- Confess Jesus Christ as Lord and Savior of your life. Nothing or no one can save you and pay the price needed to redeem you from a life of sin and separation from God. (Romans 10:9)

Truly I tell you, people can be forgiven all their sins and every slander they utter …

Mark 3:28

I humbly welcome the act of forgiveness in my life. Without it I would not know how to fall at the feet of Christ and walk in His light. Forgiveness is not based on the magnitude of sin, but on the magnitude of the forgiver's **love**. No sin is too great for God's complete and unconditional love. Forgiveness means that God looks at me as though I had never sinned. I am blameless before God.

Whoever is forgiven of much must forgive much. I *choose* to forgive daily.

CHAPTER 13

AS YOU WAIT ON YOUR BOAZ

Most people know the story of Ruth. Allow me to give you a brief summary. Ruth, a young widow, had a heart of faithfulness toward God. Ruth was a despised Moabite woman with no money, and no wealth or husband to care for her. God showed His faithfulness to Ruth by bringing her Boaz, a generous, wealthy man who rewarded her for her faithfulness in service to her mother-in-law Naomi through hard work and companionship.

By right, she could have left and pursued a better life on her on terms. Instead, she chose to honor Naomi and glean from her wisdom. Although everything was stacked against Ruth, she remained strong in character toward God. As a result, she found favor with God and Boaz, her kinsman redeemer, and ultimately found the reward of a husband.

While waiting on your Boaz these are things to consider:

- Trust that God's timing is perfect.

- Allow God to be the most important person in your life.
- Act in obedience to God.
- Mediate on your Word daily.
- Pray throughout the day.
- Make sure your prayers are not always self-centered.
- Recognize that being alone does not mean you are unlovable.
- Get active in your church home.
- Join a singles ministry.
- Enjoy time with God allowing Him to pursue you.
- Spend time getting to know yourself and learning how to love you.
- Surround yourself with positive people.
- Maintain personal boundaries to prevent compromising situations.
- Find a wise person to hold you accountable as you maintain your chastity.
- Only watch things on television that will purify your heart.
- Desire what Christ desires.
- Travel, get a hobby, go to school or get involved in activities that help you grow as a person.
- Take time out for yourself and do something you've always wanted to do.

- Read books that are geared toward embracing your singleness.
- Don't waste your time on men who are not truly embodying the Word of God.
- Have a girls' night out.
- Forgive those who may have wronged you in the past.
- Make amends to those from prior relationships, if necessary.
- Recite, memorize or post scriptures of encouragement.
- Be assured that God is faithful no matter what.
- Do not hesitate to get counseling to work through your issues.

CHAPTER 14

THINGS TO CONSIDER RATHER THAN – WHY ME?

We often place blame on our childhood and how rough it was to survive. Consider Job and how he survived even through the toughest times. Yes, he did curse his birthright, but so did I. We have all experienced rough times in our lives. Job trusted God even without all the answers.

The question many of us ask is, "Why me?" The answer is, God is preparing you for something great and powerful. It is through suffering that our faith has a chance to truly grow and God be magnified.

When you are facing difficult times, here are some things to consider:

- Stop blaming others for the way you are.
- Stop depending on yourself. You will fail. WAIT ON GOD.
- Stop letting others steal your joy.
- Allow the Spirit to work in and through you.
- Pray without ceasing.

- Choose to love as God loves.
- Read the Word of God for guidance.
- Help someone else gain strength in their struggle.
- Be aware of your faults and address them according to Scripture.
- Talk to a friend that is living victoriously and can hold you accountable.

CHAPTER 15

SUPPORT AND ACCOUNTABILITY FROM FRIENDS AND FAMILY

We all need support of people who are truly members fighting for the same body, people who hold us accountable for our actions, and will sacrifice anything to see us walk upright again as brothers and sisters in Christ. I have had my share of disappointments and long roads, but nothing I have endured compares to the suffering inflicted upon Christ. Through my tough times, God has always sent His best advisors my way with strength, wisdom, and encouragement.

In many places the Bible speaks of encouragement and strong friendships that are not easily broken. Ruth and Naomi experienced a strong friendship due to the fact that God played a significant role in their relationship. Ruth did not know much about God until she met Naomi. Naomi and Ruth were an encouragement to one another in the midst of personal struggles.

It is very easy for us to get caught up in worrying about our present problems. Through these actions we often never allow anyone to show us what true friendship in Christ is all about. We risk becoming proud and foolish not realizing that we need encouragement and advice. Scripture has much to say about foolish people who lack wisdom.

> *The way of a fool is right in his own eyes, but a wise man listens to advice.*

> ## *Proverbs 12:15 NASB*

The following pages are heart-felt words from those who have shown me the love of Christ even when I did not think I deserved it. Their encouragement and honesty helped to bring me to my knees in repentance. It is important for me to be able to hear true ministers of the Word of God minister to me in the time of need. I never realized how I too am an encouragement to others, and they needed me strong because my gift was great.

Solomon Bass- A Big Brother That Never Let Up

Cold hearted is never the answer sis. What you need to do is use wisdom and discretion when you decide to open up to someone. In all thy ways acknowledge Him and He shall direct your path, that's what our Father says to do. Do you seek God before you open your heart to others? Many times we can become impatient and just start doing our own thing, but God tells us that we need to acknowledge Him in all things. Even in friendships. It can be dangerous when we talk out of our emotions. We can end up putting ourselves in bad situations that we will later regret. Let me encourage you to MOVE along and not hold on to what happened in the past, it is not healthy. You need to be thanking God for revealing the truth. You are a beautiful woman and men are going to fall head over heels for you, but just wait and let God do His thing. His timing is perfect, sis.

You are a true meaning of the Proverbs 31 woman. I have seen many young women lose hold of who they are because of their struggles. You need to hold on to God's unchanging hand. God has given you many gifts and talents and not one have you buried. Continue to shine your light. Just as you have supported so many others in their projects the Lord will definitely fill your cup with more than enough. Your BIG BRO is proud of you!

Bobby Magee, Jr. - A Friend Like No Other

CeCe, what words can I employ to describe the depth of your character? Your pure heart and affinity towards God's people is boundless, your love for God and His Word, insurmountable, and your passion for divinity, unprecedented. Despite the brevity of our friendship, your unconditional love and support for me cannot be questioned. Woman of God you embody holiness and purity, and the level of your virtue is immeasurable. Blessed and favored are you among women for your faithfulness to the Lord. I truly believe that you have a unique gift for meeting the needs of people with proficiency and integrity.

God has great things in store for you if you continue to submit yourself to Him. I pray that you keep your mind focused and fixed on Him and that you be lead by the Holy Spirit in all of your endeavors. Do not ever allow yourself to be overwhelmed with fear. Stand strong and be of good courage. He who has begun a good work in you shall perform it until the day of Jesus.

Devon Price- Brother in Christ Holding Me Accountable

When I met you, I loved the fire that you have towards the Kingdom Agenda. In getting to know you, I have grown to see the light in you. You are very attractive, and have a lot going for yourself. I think that you have a lot of potential to be a great woman of God! But, I don't think you recognize how great. I think that the people and situations you allow around you reveal that you don't place a high value on yourself, or your position in Christ. There are many people that I have to fellowship with because we are believers, but I don't have to subject myself to any type of situation, that would question a genuine friendship. I want to let you know that you are better than that.

I am proud of you! The devil has tried to break you and lead you astray. He has tried to distract you and keep you from what the Lord has in his will for you, and he has tried to use the insecurities of your past to keep you from reaching your potential. And most of all he has tried to use one of the most powerful assets we have – the Body of Christ – to bring you down. But, you have endured it all. You have truly been an example of Romans 8:31-39. You have slipped and fallen, but you have gotten back up. You have felt sorrow and cried, but have found Joy in the morning. You have made the mistake that we all have made by putting your trust in man, but once again you used wisdom to reconnect with God for support.

So I want to encourage you to keep on making yourself available for the Lord. Keep letting him use you for a vessel to glorifying his Holy name. Keep him in the forefront of whatever you are doing and He will receive the Glory and manifest His will for your life. I want to encourage you to reflect on the forgiveness from our Lord and Savior Jesus Christ on our iniquities, and cast that same forgiveness to those who have meaningfully hurt you. I encourage you to stay in prayer, and continue in your relentless act of seeking the Lord's face and counsel. Have "crazy" faith – the faith beyond measure that the Lord will effectively use for the Kingdom Agenda.

Congratulations on your current endeavor, and know that I am here for anything that you need, and I will be praying for your continued success!

Ambriell Washington- A True Friend In God

I want to first take the time to congratulate you on the woman that you have become. We only met two years ago, but I feel I have known you for years. I know your past, and I have seen where your future is going. Make sure you continue to take the necessary strides forward to secure your dreams and passions. God has crafted you uniquely. Acknowledge that and continue to live life purposefully, and with His will in mind. Never stop. Ciarra, your presence has affected many around you in more ways than you will never know. I can tell you from my personal experience you have changed how I view life tremendously. Now I realize that every day of life is precious, and that I too can change for the better. I force myself to step aside from each situation and ask myself how the other person feels; this is something that I had a hard time doing before. I thank you Ciarra, for giving me that gift in life. Always stay true to you!

Shamille Tatum- A Sister Of Counsel

Black, pretty, strong, intelligent, and most importantly spiritual are just a few characteristics that describe you! I just want to say I am proud of where you are today as a woman of Christ. You have faced many obstacles in your life and you have illustrated to people that with the help of God, you can conquer anything. Looking back at your high school years, Ciarra, you have been able to overcome lustful and unhealthy behavior, such as drinking. Now, you are a Proverbs lady and you are growing stronger with the Lord. May God continue to bless you and use you as a tool to help others. I truly love you and I pray that you continue down this path!

Andrea Fatoma- A Transparent Sista

I used to think I could handle myself and trusted in

my own intelligence and ability to 'read' people. I felt like no guy could pull the wool over my eyes because I knew 'the games." God had to show me that every situation has a behind-the-scenes spiritual battle. The enemy of our souls is constantly going about the earth like a starving lion, searching for one of us to spiritually devour. The fact of the matter is that I am no match for the devil - God is. I've been on this earth for a mere 20-something years and the devil has been around since before this world began. Once again, I am no match. God Almighty, however, has always been-before the concept of time was even conceived. He created time, He created this world, and He created you and me. That being said, look upward, not inward. Seek wise counsel, after first seeking God.

Now, whenever I meet a guy and I find that I have the slightest interest in him, I go straight to God in prayer. That prayer goes like this: "If this man has been sent to be a stumbling block, a temptation, or a danger, please make him disappear and I won't ask any questions or make any attempt to contact him. If his presence in my life remains, as I seek Your face daily, show me what role he's been sent to play in my life. As I listen carefully to Your voice, lead and guide me according to Your will."

I encourage you to say this same prayer with all sincerity. The Bible says in **Psalm 119:1,1** *"Thy word have I hid in mine heart, that I might not sin against thee."*

Hide this *word* in your heart:

Trust in the LORD with all thine heart; and lean not unto thine own understanding. In all thy ways acknowledge him, and he shall direct thy paths. Be not wise in thine own eyes: fear the LORD, and depart from evil.

Proverbs 3:5-7

My Response to the Encouragement I Received

As I read the words of my dear friends and family, I am at awe from the number of lives I have been graciously allowed to influence and who have influenced me. At this point in my life, I have come to realize that nothing can separate me from walking in God's will. Looking back upon the adversity I faced throughout my years, I wish I would have had someone there to talk with about my problems. I buried them deep within me and took them out on innocent people. They have shown me that life does not end due to struggles and troubled times; it keeps going. Whatever God allows me to provide for others will continue to be my focus.

Therefore, since we are surrounded by such a great cloud of witnesses, let us throw off everything that hinders and the sin that so easily entangles, and let us run with perseverance the race marked out for us.

Hebrews 12:1

I am honored to take on the role as a disciple of Christ, leading people to His Kingdom.

CHAPTER 16

MY LETTER TO GOD
Ciarra's Psalm

Could I choose to be love and give love? Yes I can. Today, I am choosing to live and be happy. Lord you have spared my life so many times in so many ways, yet many times have I disappointed you with my petty desires. From this day forward I no longer want a man to be the center of my attention but only you.

I will walk through whatever door you open. I will learn to love and appreciate myself, because you do.

Lord, there is so much I want to show you. There is so much I have learned, your Word has been my rock, my shield, and protected me from physical death. I have no choice but to be grateful.

You have shown me the true meaning of love like no other. You have wrapped me in your arms and held me since birth. You never gave up on me even when I gave up on myself.

You have been my Father, my Husband and my Best Friend. In my darkest hours, You have been my Hope. I treasure You in my heart - deep within my soul. I will treasure You in everything I do. Lord, I am no longer feeding on attention from men, my attention is only focused on You. I will no longer pursue another man for my focus has become being pursued by You, the Lover of my soul.

From this moment, I desire to cast all my cares on you. This day, I choose to embrace my singleness with a smile and allow You to be the man of my life **for life,** until you bless and present your choice for me during my life's journey. Even then, you remain my highest priority. I am confident this will be possible because of Your love for me.

> *But seek first His kingdom and His righteousness, and all these things will be added to you.*

Matthew 6:3

AFTERWORD

As you read my testimony, *Season of Singleness*, I pray and hope you were inspired and encouraged. Hold on to God, and know that your strength comes from Him. No matter how tough this life gets, God is with you always. Nothing can separate you from His undying love.

The Father wants you to stand through adversity, not letting the enemy defeat you. Do not let sin control the way you live. Be willing to face your lustful desires with the Word as your sword. Provisions have already been made for your success. Keep on praying, fasting and reciting scripture. Allow and trust God to be your **ALL IN ALL**.

To Women:

We all have this desire for love and affection. God wants to meet that desire. Allow God to come in and show you true love. Know that you are a virtuous, capable, woman of God who deserves nothing but the best. Know your **worth**. God has His hand on you.

To Men:

You were made first and in the likeness of God. So walk in every aspect of the Kingdom and show yourself approved. If you want to follow Christ you have to **mimic** Christ. Focus on becoming the man of God you are called to be.

Message to All:

GOD is removing all those of importance from you that are not in His perfect will for your life. The pain they cause you cannot remain. When He does remove them, the detachment is so powerful it feels as if you are being betrayed. But, you are not. You are being strengthened and refined like precious metal. Wait upon the Lord and He will renew your strength (**Isaiah 40:31**).

> *We also pray that you will be strengthened with all his glorious power so you will have all the endurance and patience you need. May you be filled with joy.*

> *Colossians 1:11*

ABOUT THE AUTHOR

Ciarra S. Leathers is an inspiring Woman of God, daughter, sister, friend, manager, performer, and encourager. She is known for her Godly lifestyle and transparent attitude. She is originally from Kansas City, Missouri but resides in Houston, Texas.

Her successes have led her to be an inspiration to others. Throughout the triumph she has faced in her own life, she has been able to touch and inspire others with her story. Ciarra has a passion to reach troubled youth and women in the faith. She has been a counselor and encourager to many who have crossed her path. She is equipped to bring out the best in women and motivate them into a deeper connection with God.

Ciarra holds a Masters in Counseling from Houston Graduate School of Theology. She also holds a Bachelors of Arts in English with a concentration in Journalism from Missouri Western State University in Saint Joseph, Missouri.

Ciarra is a counselor to foster children in need, currently working as a managing partner for Von Won. Her mission is to reach everyone with the Gospel of Christ, exposing the enemy while glorifying the Kingdom of God. Her heart-felt desire is that everyone will walk in the likeness of Christ.

To contact the author for encouragement, speaking engagements, and other requests, please contact her via email at **Jesusluvsme_13@msn.com**

ACKNOWLEDGEMENTS

I am very thankful for my mother. She has been my rock throughout my life. She taught me the definition of a mother and a father. I am blessed to be called her daughter. I am also thankful for my grandmother, a woman of pure strength; she raised me to be an outstanding woman of God, and for my aunt Carolyn who took me in and saw something in me that I didn't see in myself. She taught me to strive beyond my expectations. I won't let you down. I'm thankful for my stepfather, Bryant who was willing to come in and raise me when my father would not. I am thankful for my Uncle Gary, and I truly appreciate his influence in my life. To my sister LaToya, I love her more than words can express, she is not only my sister but one of my closest friends. I love you Paris, she is auntie's china doll, and I love you too Brandie. I am thankful for my brother Ryan who has inspired me in so many ways, everything I am doing is because of you. You've taught me so much about loving others despite of. I'm thankful for my sister Angel, who has been a big part of my life whether she realizes it or not. Thanks to all of my aunts, uncles and cousins , and to Shamile for being a listening ear. I love all of you. I am thankful for my god parents, Mr. and Mrs. Banks. I love them for everything they taught me. I miss Mr. Banks because he showed me the true definition of a Father. I'm thankful for my god brothers and sisters. They all hold a special place in my heart.

I am thankful for The Beacon Light Seventh Day Adventist Church Family for loving me and cherishing me, and for the calling on my life. Without the truth and the ear of God I would not know how to humbly come to The Father in prayer. To my Pastor Ross and his lovely wife, who have taught me the Divine Word each Sabbath, and have supported my endeavors since the beginning. The fruit they bear shows the love of Christ. I am blessed to have grown and experience love like no other at Beacon Light. Continue to serve and be a blessing to others, like you are to me. Beacon Light will always be my home church no matter where I go. I love my Beacon Light Seven Day Adventist Church Family. Sister Gloria, thank you, too.

To all of my friends within the Body of Christ those who have held me accountable for my actions, To my sister Andrea, who has been a tremendous blessing in my life, and has been there through all of my struggles and still remained a faithful friend, always keeping it real. Ambriell, thanks for being a friend that I could always count on. Thanks, Gina for your kind words and prayers. My brother Solomon (Solo), thanks for supporting me and never giving up on me, thanks for being a Godly big brother. To my friend Bobby, thanks for sharing your wisdom and seeing my worth. I love you. Devon (Chev Dev), thanks for holding me accountable and never holding back. I appreciate your support. To my best friend Victoria, thanks for introducing me to a true growing Body of Believers. I'm so grateful. I love you chica. To Stephanie and Dr. Bradley Smith, you two have been such a blessing in my life like no other, and have inspired me to write again and to continue living out the meaning of a Christian woman. Thanks for helping me with my book and reading, editing, marketing, promoting and publishing. Thanks Von Won for the support and prayers. Thanks for believing in me and being a blessing in my life. To the Metropolitan Seventh Day Adventist Church Family, thank you for accepting me as one of your own. You have opened my eyes to a new meaning of fellowship. Thanks for the support, prayers and phone calls when I miss church. Pastor and Mrs. Baysa thanks for your willingness to come out and have Bible study with me, and for potluck and making me feel at home. Jenny, Betty, and Michelle, I love you women of God.

Thanks to the many that were not named, and know that I am thankful for the prayers, support, and love you have displayed. THANK YOU!!

APPENDIX I.

Frequently Asked Questions ...
Following God When Circumstances are Overwhelming

1. Could I come to God, even after salvation, when I have fallen?

Yes. The Bible states that we've all sinned and have fallen short of the glory of God. The Bible also talks about nothing separating us from the love of God. Nothing we do can cause us to be completely separated from God. Come to Him with a repentant heart and He will forgive.

Romans 3:23

Romans 8:38-39

Mark 3:28-29

2. How can I deal with my lustful desires?

God created desires in everyone. We are responsible to make sure our desires are directed in the right direction. When we commit our mind to Christ our focus and desires will change. God will give you a renewed Spirit and a desire for His Word. The Bible tells us that if we delight ourselves in the Lord, He will give us the desires of our heart (Psalm 37:4). This means that He will place desires in our heart as we commit to delight in Him.

Philippians 4:8

Galatians 5:17

Romans 7: 5-6

3. Does being single mean that God doesn't love me?

Singleness, in light of poor relationships, is a gift from God. Embrace it and know that God loves you. When you start to feel sorry for yourself, that's when the enemy attacks you with sin. Be wise and know that God values you. Be content in whatever God gives you.

Psalm 139:17

Philippians 4:11

1 Corinthians 7:32-34

4. How can I distinguish love from lust?

Love does what is right in the sight of God. Lust only lurks from the enemy. Love does not lie nor is love rude or disrespectful. The object and purpose of love is to act in the Will of God.

1 Corinthians 13:4-7

1 Timothy 1:5

Romans 12:9

5. What does forgiveness mean? How can I forgive?

Forgiveness is accepting the faults of others as an act of the enemy. Forgiveness means opening up your heart to forgive because God forgave you. Forgiveness frees you from the hold that the other person has over you.

Forgiveness paves the way for healthier relationships.

Matthew 5:44

Matthew 6:14

Ephesians 1:7

6. Does forgiving someone mean you have to forget?

Forgiving someone doesn't mean you magically get amnesia. You forgive never to bring it up again because your heart has let go and allowed God to work.

Luke 6: 37

Matthew 6:12

2 Peter 1:9

7. Can I pray for patience?

There's an old saying that my former Pastor used to say, "Don't pray for patience because patience brings about tribulations." Whatever the affliction, tribulation or trial, God will deliver you from them all. Don't get impatient, but rather focus on God's strength. We must wait patiently on God knowing that His timing is perfect.

Psalm 40:1

Galatians 5:22

Romans 8:24-25

8. Why can't I pursue a man?

The Bible tells woman to allow the man to pursue you. Allow God to pursue your heart and give you His desires.

Proverbs 18:22

9. Does prayer work?

Yes, prayer works if your mind is truly humbled in prayer. Prayer is your communication with God. Through prayer we learn active worship.

Mark 1:35

Psalm 9:1-2

Matthew 6:5-13

10. How can I deal with self-esteem issues?

God made us in His image. This mean we are all beautiful in God's eye. God loves us so much that he placed value on each one of us. God promises us a long life with Him when we believe in His goodness. It is unhealthy to have low self-esteem. When we do we doubt God's goodness. Let's value ourselves as God values us.

Romans 12:3

Psalm 139:13-16

1 Corinthians 6:19-20

APPENDIX II.

Scriptures To Keep You Focused On God

Not only so, but we also glory in our sufferings, because we know that suffering produces perseverance; perseverance, character; and character, hope.

Romans 5:3-4

This section will help you face your fears and heartaches. These are helpful scriptures that I needed when life became overwhelming. Allow the Holy Spirit to guide you through your pain knowing that suffering brings about strength.

Abandonment

Though my father and mother forsake me, the LORD will receive me.

Psalms 27:10

Keep your lives free from the love of money and be content with what you have, because God has said, "Never will I leave you; never will I forsake you."

Hebrews 13:5

A father to the fatherless, a defender of widows, is God in his holy dwelling.

Psalms 68:5

Let us then approach God's throne of grace with confidence, so that we may receive mercy and find grace to help us in our time of need.

Hebrews 4:16

"I am God, the God of your father," he said. "Do not be afraid to go down to Egypt, for I will make you into a great nation there."

Genesis 46:3

Crucifixion with Christ

Those who belong to Christ Jesus have crucified the flesh with its passions and desires.

Galatians 5:24

From now on, let no one cause me trouble, for I bear on my body the marks of Jesus.

Galatians 6:17

I have been crucified with Christ and I no longer live, but Christ lives in me. The life I now live in the body, I live by faith in the Son of God, who loved me and gave himself for me.

Galatians 2: 20

Forgiveness

Truly I tell you, people can be forgiven all their sins and every slander they utter, but whoever blasphemes against the Holy Spirit will never be forgiven; they are guilty of an eternal sin.

Mark 3:28-29

And forgive us our debts, as we also have forgiven our debtors.

Matthew 6:12

And when you stand praying, if you hold anything against anyone, forgive them, so that your Father in heaven may forgive you your sins.

Mark 11:25-26

Be kind and compassionate to one another, forgiving each other, just as in Christ God forgave you.

Ephesians 4:32

For if you forgive other people when they sin against you, your heavenly Father will also forgive you. But if you do not forgive others their sins, your Father will not forgive your sins.

Matthew 6:14-15

Love

For God so loved the world that he gave his one and only Son, that whoever believes in him shall not perish but have eternal life.

John 3:16

Love the Lord your God with all your heart and with all your soul and with all your mind and with all your strength.

Mark 12:30

But I tell you, love your enemies and pray for those who persecute you.

Matthew 5:44

But God demonstrates his own love for us in this: While we were still sinners, Christ died for us.

Romans 5:8

For you know the grace of our Lord Jesus Christ, that though he was rich, yet for your sake he became poor, so that you through his poverty might become rich.

2 Corinthians 8:9

And hope does not put us to shame, because God's love has been poured out into our hearts through the Holy Spirit, who has been given to us.

Romans 5:5

Neither height nor depth, nor anything else in all creation, will be able to separate us from the love of God that is in Christ Jesus our Lord.

Romans 8:39

Love is patient, love is kind. It does not envy, it does not boast, it is not proud. It does not dishonor others, it is not self-seeking, it is not easily angered, it keeps no record of wrongs. Love does not delight in evil but rejoices with the truth. It always protects, always trusts, always hopes, always perseveres.

1 Corinthians 13:4-7

Repentance

Godly sorrow brings repentance that leads to salvation and leaves no regret, but worldly sorrow brings death.

2 Corinthians 7:10

You do not delight in sacrifice, or I would bring it; you do not take pleasure in burnt offerings. My sacrifice, O God, is a broken spirit; a broken and contrite heart you, God, will not despise.

Psalms 51:16-17

Now there were some present at that time who told Jesus about the Galileans whose blood Pilate had mixed with their sacrifices. Jesus answered, "Do you think that these Galileans were worse sinners than all the other Galileans because they suffered this way? I tell you no! But unless you repent, you too will all perish. Or those eighteen who died when the tower in Siloam fell on them — do you think they were more guilty than the others living in Jerusalem? I tell you, no! But unless you repent, you too will all perish."

Luke 13:1-5

Restoration

He himself bore our sins" in his body on the cross, so that we might die to sins and live for righteousness; "by his wounds you have been healed."

1 Peter 2:24

Come to me, all you who are weary and burdened, and I will give you rest.

Matthew 11:28

But he was pierced for our transgressions, he was crushed for our iniquities; the punishment that brought us peace was on him, and by his wounds we are healed.

Isaiah 53:5

Not only is this so, but we also boast in God through our Lord Jesus Christ, through whom we have now received reconciliation.

Romans 5:11

For to be sure, he was crucified in weakness, yet he lives by God's power. Likewise, we are weak in him, yet by God's power we will live with him in our dealing with you. Examine yourselves to see whether you are in the faith; test yourselves. Do you not realize that Christ Jesus is in you—unless, of course, you fail the test? And I trust that you will discover that we have not failed the test. Now we pray to God that you will not do anything wrong—not so that people will see that we have stood the test but so that you will do what is right even though we may seem to have failed.

2 Corinthians 13:4-7

Singleness

An unmarried woman or virgin is concerned about the Lord's affairs: Her aim is to be devoted to the Lord in both body and spirit. But a married woman is concerned about the affairs of this world—how she can please her husband.

1 Corinthians 7:34

But I wish everyone were single, just as I am. But God gives to some Season of marriage, and to others Season of singleness.

1 Corinthians 7: 7 NLT

Worthy

You were bought at a price. Therefore honor God with your bodies.

1 Corinthians 6:20

He heals the brokenhearted and binds up their wounds.

Psalms 147:3

You were bought at a price. Therefore honor God with your bodies.

1 Corinthians 6:20

He heals the brokenhearted and binds up their wounds.

Psalms 147:3

A wife of noble character who can find? She is worth far more than rubies. Her husband has full confidence in her and lacks nothing of value. She brings him good, not harm, all the days of her life. She selects wool and flax and works with eager hands. She is like the merchant ships, bringing her food from afar. She gets up while it is still night; she provides food for her family and portions for her female servants. She considers a field and buys it; out of her earnings she plants a vineyard. She sets about her work vigorously; her arms are strong for her tasks. She sees that her trading is profitable, and her lamp does not go out at night. In her hand she holds the distaff and grasps the spindle with her fingers. She opens her arms to the poor and extends her hands to the needy. When it snows, she has no fear for her household; for all of them are clothed in scarlet. She makes coverings for her bed; she is clothed in fine linen and purple. Her husband is respected at the city gate, where he takes his seat among the elders of the land. She makes linen garments and sells them, and supplies the merchants with sashes. She is clothed with strength and dignity; she can laugh at the days to come. She speaks with wisdom, and faithful instruction is on her tongue. She watches over the affairs of her household and does not eat the bread of idleness. Her children arise and call her blessed; her husband also, and he praises her: "Many women do noble things, but you surpass them all." Charm is deceptive, and beauty is fleeting; but a woman who fears the LORD is to be praised. Honor her for all that her hands have done, and let her works bring her praise at the city gate.

Proverbs 31

SUGGESTED READING

Bowlby, J. *A Secure Base*. New York, NY: Basic Books, 1988.

Bowlby, J. *Attachment and Loss: Vol. 1*. New York, NY: Basic Books, 1969.

Crawford, Na'Kisha. *So Good It Hurts: The Fight. The Pain. The Love*. Lubbock, TX: Pathway Publishing, 2008.

Meyer, Joyce. *Beauty for Ashes*. New York, NY: Warner Books, 1994.

Meyer, Joyce. *Living Beyond Your Feelings: Controlling Emotions So They Don't Control You*. New York, NY: Faith Words, 2011.

McMenamin, Cindi. *Letting God Meet Your Emotional Needs*. Eugene, OR: Harvest House Publishers, 2000.

McMenamin, Cindi. *When God Pursues a Woman's Heart*. Eugene, OR: Harvest House Publishers, 2003.

McMenamin, Cindi. *When Women Walk Alone: Finding Strength and Hope Through the Seasons of Life.* Eugene, OR: Harvest House Publishers, 2002.

Schlessinger, Laura, Dr. *Bad Childhood, Good Life.* New York, NY: HarperCollins, 2006.

Schlessinger, Laura, Dr. *Surviving a Shark Attack (on Land): Overcoming Betrayal and Dealing with Revenge.* New York, NY: HarperCollins, 2011.

HOTLINES

Name	Toll-Free Number
Child Abuse and Neglect	1.800.392.3738
Domestic Violence	1.800.799.7233 (SAFE)
Sexual Assault	1.800.656.4673 (HOPE)
Drug and Alcohol Hotline	1.800.521.7128
National Suicide Prevention Lifeline	1.800.273.8255 (TALK)
National Runaway Switchboard	1.800.621.4000
National Center for Exploited Children	1.800.843.5678
National Child Abuse Hotline	1.800.252.2873 (ABUSE)
National Youth Crisis Hotline	1.800.448.4663
America's Pregnancy Hotline	1.888.672.2296
Anti-Hate Line (Discrimination)	1.800.649.0404
Self-Injury	1.800.366.8288 (DON'T CUT)

www.ingramcontent.com/pod-product-compliance
Lightning Source LLC
LaVergne TN
LVHW021537080426
835509LV00019B/2699